In the Meantime

Yvonne A. Rupende

Sunesis Ministries

In the Meantime

Copyright © 2014 Yvonne A. Rupende

The right of Yvonne A. Rupende to be identified as the author of this work has been asserted by her in accordance with the Copyright, Designs, and Patents Act 1988.

The author guarantees all contents are original and do not infringe upon the legal rights of any other person or work. All rights reserved. No part of this publication may be reproduced or transmitted in any form or by any means, electronic or mechanical, including photocopy, recording, or any information storage and retrieval system, without permission in writing from the author.

Scripture quotations marked (ESV) are from The Holy Bible, English Standard Version®, copyright © 2001 by Crossway, a publishing ministry of Good News Publishers. Used by permission. All rights reserved.

Scripture quotations marked "NIV" are taken from THE HOLY BIBLE, NEW INTERNATIONAL VERSION®, NIV® Copyright © 1973, 1978, 1984, 2011 by Biblica, Inc.® Used by permission. All rights reserved worldwide.

Scripture quotations marked "NKJV" quotations are from the Holy Bible, New King James Version Copyright © 1982 Thomas Nelson, Inc. Used by permission. All rights reserved.

Scripture quotations marked "KJV" are taken from the Holy Bible, King James Version.

The views expressed in this book are solely those of the author and do not necessarily reflect the views of the publisher, and the publisher herby disclaims any responsibility for them. The author accepts sole legal responsibility for the contents of this book.

ISBN: 978-0-9928495-7-3

Sunesis Ministries

Website of publisher:

WWW.STUARTPATTICO.COM

Contents

Book Dedication 7
On My Knees 11
Let It Be 12
Why Didn't I Believe? 13
Look at Me 15
Lord of the Dance 17
How Long Lord? 19
Promise of Victory 21
Mercy and Honour 23
Prisoner of Love 24
I Have Died So Many Times 25
Healing the Wounds of the Past 26
No Escape 28
Touched 30
All Glory 32
The Sheep and The Shepherd 34
Reminiscence 36
Spiritual Healing 40
In the Meantime 42
Dreams 45

Seven Times He Said Go Again	46
Thoughts of God	48
I Will Pray Tomorrow	50
Warrior Power	52
No More	54
My Purpose	55
Mind Trap	56
Night Time	58
The Pain	60
Strike Back	63
What Was That?	64
It's All About Me	66
Thank You	69
Desert Storm	71
All Is Well With My Soul	73
Super Natural	74
The New Has Come	75
Flourish like a Palm tree	77
I Would Rather Be A Doorkeeper	78
Innocence of Youth	80
What Would It Be like?	82
Good Day, Holy Spirit	84
Exceptional Favour	86
Blessed and Highly Favoured	87
On the Cusp of the Hill	89
Earthen Vessel	92
It's Already Done	93
Tell the Devil	94

Absent Prayer 95
Limitless 96
Muddy Haze 98
Whose Race? 100
Dry Bones & Her Staff 101
Not Today 103
Us 104
Noisy Place 105
Confusion to Calm 107
Stay Here 108
Impasse 109
All For Me 111
Mr. Down Tools 113
My Plans in Disarray 115
Hate, Dissipate 117
Glory to Glory 119

Book Dedication

This book is dedicated to my mother, father, grandparents, children and husband.

My grandmother and mother have been the stimuli behind this literature. Their creative gene has been passed down throughout the family: my grandmother the playwright; my mother the story writer; my brother and sons - gifted musicians and story writers in the making. No longer shall I hide our light under a bushel. Instead, I illuminate the gift of the Creator in the hope of blessing those coming through after me.

I also thank my beloved husband and children for their continuous support, love and encouragement. They are my greatest encouragers and cheerleaders.

I would also like to thank my beautiful sister in Christ, Mrs. Jenny Wilson, for pressing me towards the mark. Thanks too, to my ever faithful brethren, for their care, love, and encouragement in my quest for spirit and truth.

Though the storms grow, I am like the palm tree; I bend but *shall not* break. The spirit of the Lord is upon me. My word shall not return to me void.

"*For as the rain comes down, and the snow from heaven, and do not return there, but water the earth, and make it bring forth and bud, that it may give seed to the sower and bread to the eater, so shall My word be that goes forth from My mouth; it shall not return to Me void, but it shall accomplish what I please, and it shall prosper in the thing for which I sent it*". *(Isaiah 55:10-11 NKJV)*

On My Knees

When I'm on my knees I'm taller than the trees,
When taller than the trees I feel His holy breeze,
When I feel His breeze I rest in His peace;
Only when I'm down on my knees.

When I'm prostrate I feel God's grace,
When I feel His grace I know I'm safe,
When I know I'm safe I can relate,
To the ones who discern my needs.

Jehovah Rapha, my One who heals.
Jehovah Shalom, my God of peace.
Jehovah Elohim, my Lord my God,
El-Shaddai, He who is sufficient for my needs.

Let It Be

Let me, oh Lord, move with grace,
Let me share the skies with the birds so great,
Let me bask in the coolness of the seas,
Let me submerge in the land and the trees,
Let me, oh Lord, let me be.

Let not thy hand fall away from me,
Let not thy eyes drift off from me,
Let not thy feet trample me,
Let not thy hand disbar me,
Let not, oh Lord, you ever leave me.

Let us walk along in the gentle breeze,
Let us tarry a while on the golden beach,
Let us speak of hope and heavenly things,
Let us commit with our wedding ring,
Let us, oh Lord, let us sing.

Why Didn't I Believe?

Why didn't I believe when He spoke to me
All those years ago in those quiet places?
He whispered in my ear, calling my name,
But I shooed Him away, I felt so ashamed.

Why did I doubt Him, did I see a ghost?
No, it was Christ Jesus walking on the ocean
With his arms outstretched to welcome me;
Still fear and doubt caused me to sink.

But My merciful Father so full of light
Rescued me from a swallowing might,
From rages, wars and the storms of life,
From the chills of the deep and a ghastly plight.

He purged, he fashioned, he mended me
From war-torn years and ravenous beasts,
He tutored, gave visions, at times scolded me
And reminded me where I could have been.

When I was able to take infant steps
There He was still, with His arms outstretched,

Nervous I was but He kept calling,
Encouraging, praising and blessing me.

I say with my heart, my soul and my mouth
That I love the Lord Jesus, on Him I can count,
My heart is filled with songs for Him,
Praise the Lord, El Shaddai, let us sing, let us sing.

So why didn't I believe as He spoke to me
Throughout the years in many, many places?
Was it fear, doubt, loss of vision, loss of faith?
"Hath not the potter power over the clay"?

I see now, Lord, how patient you've been,
The countless times you stepped right in
And rescued me from the withering plights
And held me close each and every night.

If I disbelieve one single day
Or doubt your whispers in my ear,
Remind me of Peter and You on the water
And this will be my guide.

Look at Me

Lord, what did you see when you looked at me?
I merely believed but still you rescued me.
My head was bowed, bloody and ashamed,
When I realised how far I fell from your grace.

I wallowed, I cried, I blamed and I prayed,
Still hid secret vengeance deep down, full of hate.
But when you sent angels of mercy in place,
They help me release those passions of hate.

Lord, you are so awesome, so powerful, so great,
It is only to you I can deeply relate.
You're my dearest, most trusted soul mate,
In the good times and the bad times, whatever my state.

You assembled an army to act as my shield
When I was so tired and ready to give in;
They fortified, counselled and comforted me,
Then placed me back into Your soft tender wings.

As I draw back the veil, Lord, look at me now,
My head is no longer bloody and bowed.

I'm no longer ashamed of where I have been,
For I know that My Lord is my Saviour and King.

So now I am joyful in my Lord,
My Maker, my Keeper, my One and all.
Life's journey is temporary, Lord's beauty I see,
Eternal and humble, assured and complete.

With the breath of life I can fight, come what may,
For I know my anointing is here to stay.
Whatever disappointments come my way,
He'll bring peace, contentment; keep me out of harm's way.

Look at me Lord, saints, look at me,
Look what Lord Jesus has done for me,
Look how far He has taken me,
Look at me now, I'm a beautiful queen.
Look at me, Lord,
Oh look at me!

Lord of the Dance

Lord, I stand in awe of your mighty outpouring of blessings upon me. I know I have been catapulted into your light and kingdom in a mighty way.

How could I run from you ever again? If I tried I could not escape your love for me. For I know you loved me from the first and will love me to the last.

In the valley, you are there, up on the mountain top, you are there, on the crest of the waves, you are there, through the storms and the rain, you are there, where there is peace and joy, you are there, upon my victory you are there.

Lord, I am overcome with delight that you favour me. My heart skips a beat when you are near. Only you are my greatest love. You are faultless, blameless, everlasting, and shower me with your magnificence.

I cannot forget the time that you kept my eyes from tears and my feet from falling. You insisted that I see your power, love, grace and mercy. How then can I not show everyone how much I love you? In your presence I am ecstatic, I sing, I dance, I unwind and find peace.

There's no one else like you who is faithful and true. My life and heart are testimonies that say you are holy, wonderful and worthy.

How Long Lord?

Lord, I call to you from my pits of despair,
Are you there, are you there, are you there?
Come down and show yourself to me,
My Lord, how I need you near.

How long, my Lord, must I look on
And see my enemies about me?
Gloating and waiting, hoping for failing -
How long, Lord, tell me, how long?

I cry out, Lord, in the hope that you hear me,
Every tear drop that falls tears my soul.
From my belly of hell, I weep and I wail,
But, Lord, you are nowhere to be found.

Oh Lord, why, oh why, do you leave me to cry?
Tell me please what I have done wrong?
Help me, Lord, give me hope, give me light to see
What I'm to do for your renewed love.

In my madness, my thoughts, I rock and I cry,
Holding in the decades of pain,

Lord, I tried and tried and tried and tried,
But I still can't release the pain.

While the world carries on
I am locked in my thoughts, wailing from deep within.
Nobody knows how I cried last night,
It's my secret that lives with me.

How long will you hide your face from me?
How long must I feel this shame?
How long must I cry and wrestle with my thoughts?
Tell me, how many more years of pain?

Lord, why can't you see the sorrow in my heart
And the groaning of my crying bones?
What of the promises that you gave to me,
Those which you sealed with love?

If it was not for the love that I have for you
I would have surely keeled over or died.
Right here I stand despite my plight,
For in You I know I will rise.

I know that you keep your promises,
So of you I ask one thing:
Lord, cradle me and give me peace,
And speak to the inner me.

Promise of Victory

Lord, where is the victory that you promised?
You told me it's on its way.
I heard this promise such a long time ago,
Only hope and faith keep me day after day.

Lord, where is victory that you promised?
How do we break down Jericho Walls?
You said I would go from defeat to victory,
But how long will I fight the cause?

Lord, where is the victory that you promised?
That victory which brings release,
You said I will go from poverty to prosperity,
And rest in your eternal peace.

Oh, now I sense victory on the horizon -
I can taste it in my mouth.
I can touch it with my hands, how amazing
I feel its aura all around.

As I rest on the victory you promised,
I feel no sense of defeat.

I feel no sense of poverty,
I see only your promise to me.

Victory, Victory, Victory is yours,
Says, the Prince of Peace.
He says, "Move by faith and trust in me.
Now, embrace your victory!"

Mercy and Honour

Mercy and Honour, those are my names,
For years I concealed them within my domain,
Those times of torture, tyranny and dismay,
It was Mercy and Honour who kept me sane.

Mercy and Honour conditioned in me,
Passed on by women who've gone on before,
When I was indignant with cause, not with blame,
It was Mercy and Honour who kept me from shame.

Mercy and Honour are given to me
By my Almighty Father whose realm I dwell in,
He teaches me patience, gives sustenance and relief,
Mercy and Honour liberated me.

Mercy and Honour, those are my names,
Thriving alongside my earthly names,
Those two names were chosen so carefully for me,
My Mercy, for those who so offended me.
My Honour, for Him who's the author of me.
Mercy and Honour, stay breathing in me.

Prisoner of Love

I am a prisoner of love,
Locked in my room,
Living in hope,
Fighting with doom;
I am a prisoner of love,
Locked in my room!

I am a patient of promise,
Of blood, sweat and tears,
I survived all those years.
I surrendered my life,
To quests I believed,
A patient of promise am I.

Prisoners of love -
Who can know them?
Rebels for love and genuineness;
Their scent of promise
Dwells on the horizon,
Prisoners of love - you'll find me there.

I Have Died So Many Times

Address me as Phoenix -
A life cycle has ended;
I now lay down to rest.
My old life has gone,
Just as the sun goes down
I return into my nest.

Fear not, my mourners,
My journey's not over,
Though I was extinguished
Before your eyes.
For out of the nest
Came a new creation,
I spread out my wings for flight.

I have died so many times,
I have died so many times,
But like the Phoenix I rise, I rise!
I have died so many times,
But I rise, still I rise,
Like the beautiful phoenix I rise!

Healing the Wounds of the Past

Healing the wounds of the past
Is a long and painful journey:
There are many brooks to cross
And many rivers to overcome.
At times we can not envisage
How and what we must do,
But if God delivered Daniel
He'll do the same for you.

Healing the wounds of the past
Can mean shouldering some of the blame.
It's hard to know where it all started
And more difficult to examine the pain.
But dry your weeping eyes, my child,
And be encouraged in your faith,
For God will bestow on you the oratory of Moses,
In Hagar's humility you'll bear no shame.

Healing the wounds of the past
Does mean stripping away all the pain
Of the times gone by, of things unresolved -
They may never be fixed again.

Just hold on to God's healing power
And all He continues to do.
If Moses, Hagar and Daniel made it
Your healing from the past will come too.

No Escape

You told me that this act of mercy
And forgiveness would happen to me.
Believe me when I tell you that
It has come in like a flood,
From every angle, every direction,
Through everything in my daily life,
Even to me in the twilight hours.

Your angels often visit me
And speak of considerable things:
Of mercy, humility, love and new life.
I see there is no escape for me.
There are no more excuses I can find,
There are no more fears to tread,
Time to stand firm and walk in my faith,
You will guide me all the way.

For the wages of sin is death -
I cannot bring this upon myself;
In truth, mercy and forgiveness
I will be set free.
And lest I forget what He has spoken

Many times to me,
Today again, He speaks and says,
"Trust me once again."

Touched

When you touch me, Lord, my spirit moves
Creating an atmosphere within this room,
As I close my eyes to capture you
My aching heart is completely soothed.

Lord, how can I expect to understand
The calling you spoke of is now at hand?
Anticipating greatness of what is to come,
Still my heart is receptive to the one I love.

I am filled with your power to do what you ask,
To be faithful and true with all that's involved
I know it's not about how well they respond;
It's about my purpose and overcoming strongholds.

I stand in strength to accomplish your will,
In the face of rebelliousness, stiff-necks
And of those that say, "Kill."
Though their hearts are hard, I will persevere;
In grief, while they talk, I'll be still in prayer.

Of the times you've told me not to be afraid
Your spirit within me erases rejection and shame.
I'm criticised for calling your name
But will stand firm in knowing your true love remains.

You say, "Digest my Word, so that I can strengthen you
And fill your faith with my Word so sweet and true.
From the inside out and the outside in,
You'll be spiritually lifted and prepared to enter in."

Your Word sinks deep within my heart,
I share Your gospel near and far,
As I grow in joy, giving thanks to You,
As I weep in the struggle you'll comfort me too.

My comfort, my strength, my carer and friend
I know you'll be with me until the end.
When you touch me, you ask, "Does not your spirit move?"
"Yes, my singing and praises fill this room."

All Glory

Bread of Life,
I want to give you all glory.
For your wondrous love to me.
I praise your name,
In everything I do.

Tree of Life,
Oh, how you blossom.
Your arms spread wide,
Encompass me and hold me tight,
I am secure in you.

Man of Promise,
Look how you've made me.
My life's fulfilled,
My heart is free from misery,
Because I believe in You.

River of dreams,
Flow deep within me.
I'm purified,
I'm running free

With quickening speed,
Through land into the sea.

Most High One,
How I exalt You.
You lift my heart,
I am in awe,
I shout for joy,
There is no one like You.

The Sheep and The Shepherd

Shepherd, where are God's blessed sheep?
Have you been taking care of yourself alone?
The sheep are lost, weak and sick,
They are scared, injured and alone.

Were you so busy that you could not be moved?
Did you not see them wandering on mountains high
Waiting to be plundered by Satan's hunters?
Shepherd, why were they left to die?

O shepherd, hear the word of the Sovereign Lord,
"I remove my sheep and will tend to them myself.
They will no longer be fodder for the devil to bother,
I will restore brightness out of their darkened days."

Wherever they step they have been heavenly blessed,
Showers of blessings descend upon them as rainy seasons.
Their lives have transformed, their strength now restored.
I marvel beyond reason, what a bountiful season!

His sheep live in peace, grazing with good food to eat,
Their lands are renowned for their pastures green.

Never will they say, "Shepherd, I am afraid."
His sheep will show the shepherd God's way,
And the shepherd will kneel and pray,
And let the Lord God have His way!

Reminiscence

Almighty God, my Heavenly Father,
You are an awesome Lord:
I cannot get over your patience and power,
I constantly shake my head.

For I remember a time
When I thought I would die
From the nonstop plagues of defeat,
When my world hit rock-bottom,
When I cursed and gave up
And You said, "No child this is not the end."

Lord God, my emotions went back and forth
And I felt I suffered long -
Living with my enemy,
Being chased by the devil;
Lord, I was running from him every night.

Satan would try me this way and that,
Use people against me, even saints from the flock.
My closest friends I felt I had lost,
Then again feeling abandon, whipped and man-handled,

I had to pray fervently again.

I'd write poems and acclaims,
Not knowing how those words
Could fall from my lips like they are now;
Feeling no shame I let them pour out like rain,
It was there my healing from pain came.

Speaking and writing to God
Was my only real love.
In Him I could be true and feel free,
Reeling off pain day after day,
Most of all I could truly be me.

I would never have said
I would be here today,
Writing, not caring for sleep.
Tonight it's really late -
Six hours' sleep now, but I need eight
To function tomorrow again.

But when I am with the Lord
Tiredness flees, where it goes I do not know,
But the spirit that's in me
Needs to say these things,
Before I fall asleep.

For His investment to shine

He first has to settle my life,
To a point where I am rested
And no longer tested,
Free of fear, tears and lies.

Slight fear I have but I am excited too,
For what the Lord has prepared for me.
But because I trust Him
And He has delivered me,
I give all authority to Him.

Recalling my pain, poverty and shame
I marvel at my journey with Him.
Joy, prosperity, respect, outpourings of love
Are restored and added to my name -
Even my enemies no longer have to be ashamed
For I forgave them along the way.

I am pleased that the Lord has recorded my journey
In this period of my life.
I was once told by a person of old
That I could never be a writer or be great,
But guess what, you see what God has made?

Awesome Lord, I exalt you forever,
Your name is great beyond measure.
I request you remain permanently in my life
And anoint my loved ones at the same time.

If they don't feel you now, one day they will -
Please do not forget this prayer that I submit:
They will receive when the time is right
And you put all their wrongs right.

I just had to share
This outpouring right here
Or else I would have wrestled in my sleep tonight.
I love you, Lord,
I thank you, Lord,
For saving this child
When she thought she'd died.

Spiritual Healing

I am touched by the presence of God
Speaking into my very soul;
I heard the devil open his mouth,
Spewing a voice of fear and confusion.
In the midst of this devil stomping,
God interjected and spoke directly to me
And said, "Spiritual healing."
.
God's word rang in my ears
As I heard the physician say,
"My drugs are medically proven to work."
I slumped in the chair gulping for air
At the prospect of the physician's options given to me.
All three drugs, each worse than the other,
They'll tie me up and I'll never be free.

"Spiritual healing," He whispered in my ear,
I am reminding you I am here.
The physician talked while God dismissed
The worst news I had ever received,
"Anti-depressant drugs for me?"
No, "Spiritual healing," God re-echoed to me.

I then bolted upright at His heavenly sight,
His presence was in the room.
The more I absorbed the words He spoke
I thought, "These physicians cannot do anything for me."
Jehovah Rapha, The One who Heals!

In the Meantime

I feel like I am in a wilderness period. My friend called it a Season of Dryness. At first I felt bad that as a Daughter of the Most High I could walk in such a way. But the more she spoke I began to see that this 'dryness' was not such a bad thing but a necessary process. The only thing I can equate it to is a bird moulting its feathers. How interesting!

This means then that I am a 'Transformer in the Lord'.

Opposites abound: there is night then day, what goes up must come down, a light switches on or off. Life is as simple as that. So then I was not at all surprised when she said that I was experiencing dryness, because God was bringing me into a new beginning. Let's rewind a moment because I believe you missed something... the word 'into'. It's like a process word. You have got to go "into" or pass through to come out the other side.

So if I am coming into a new beginning, what does this mean to me? I cannot see what is different in this dry period. I know what God has done and what he has told me He is going to do: I have a check list. I am not despairing but I just feel a sense of nothingness or dryness at this time. I have not given up on God, no never. I just am not praying and reading scripture like I ought to, in actual fact like I want to. I am not in fellowship like before. I am finding reasons for not going to the house of God and, believe me, I can justify them. But when you place your excuses (called reasons) before Him they are not important. What is in your heart and where your heart is, are what God is going to counsel you over.

But where has this sense of dryness come from, this nothingness? I feel I am off track. I feel I am being diverted. In actual fact I have just experienced this as I am writing. The devil knows when to come and make an entrance. But, devil, know this... the way is shut! Praise the Lord. I also feel like I am in the wilderness. There are people around me, but what do we have in common? Where have all my Holy Ghost-filled brothers and sisters gone? Surely, the House of the Lord is not the only meeting place? My living room is open to receive the Holy Spirit with those who want to delve ocean-deep into the Word.

Through our conversation God started to talk to me. To let Him know I have heard Him, I look to the heavens and say, "Thank you Lord" or "I hear you Lord."

He was also speaking through my friend. She said that because I am coming 'into' this new 'Season of Development' I have to get rid of all the distractions, some not necessarily bad, but distractions nonetheless. I have to separate or cut ties with the things holding me back. But what if you do not know what they are? Then what? All I can do is put these questions and matters before God.

But what do I do in the meantime? You wait patiently on the Lord. Let Him have His way and do His will. As sure as there is night and day you shall receive clarity. The apostle Paul said "...I press towards the mark..." (Philippians 3: 14 KJV) This is what God expects you and me to do: "Keep your eyes on the prize." "Be still, and know that I am God." (Psalms 46: 10 NIV)

When you are wondering where He is, or just need an update, ask Him. He is not callous; he is just the opposite, compassionate and loving.

Dreams

Lord, when you called me
And I did not hear you,
You came to me again.
When I did not receive you completely
You came back to me again.
On the third time you came
I only heard your rustling:
The fourth time you came,
I was distracted.

One night I was watching TV alone,
When you jolted me unexpectedly,
I cried aloud and fell prostrate at your feet.
Like a meteor confirmation came to me, saying,
"Child, rise and claim your destiny,
Make those dreams you have become reality.
You cannot recoil now,
Your plans have been confirmed,
Here is your time of victory.
I will anoint you with clarity,
This is your time,
Your dreams are alive."

Seven Times He Said Go Again

Lord, I thank you for the many times that I fell and you raised me. You told me to stand up and look towards the sea, but in so doing I saw nothing but a never-ending expanse of water. Again, you called me to look and still I found nothing. Nevertheless, every day you would send me. Then one day I saw a light, as small as a pinhead, shining intensely upon me.

I saw a cloud as small as a human hand rising out of the sea. I cried "Lord what is this?" You told me to *get up and go.*

In preparing myself for the journey, I thank you for directing me to, *"...go down before the rain stops you"* (1 Kings 18:44 NIV), to depart before the building crumbles.

Your persistence towards me paid off and I thank you, Lord, for not allowing me to miss the small miracles and celebrations waiting for me. Had I missed those, then I would have lost out on the bigger miracles and celebrations that are also essential to my future, so I thank you, Lord.

"Now unto him that is able to keep you from falling and present you faultless before the presence of his glory with exceeding joy. (Jude 1:24 KJV)

You invested much time in me. We have had some marathon journeys. My flesh knew not when these journeys would end. These marathon journeys and challenges became countless, tiring, and tearful. I called on you many times to give me the strength to keep pressing on and you did. In return, I could only keep my faith and never lose my hope and praise in you. It is good that you were in charge of our journey because this flesh would have given up. I would have listened to Job's wife, *"... Curse God and die." (Job 2:9 KJV)*

Notwithstanding, I stand as a child of Christ and declare 'in the name of Jesus, that I was obedient, faithful, steadfast and of the Lord. My time was in Your hands. When I stumbled and fell near the finishing line you were standing there at the sidelines as my cheerleader. At the finishing line you were my coach telling me to get up from my hands and knees, "It's time to go, your time is now."

Wow, every time I cross the finishing line of one of your races, I shout out to you with a voice of triumph and lift up my hands in worship. To God be the glory great things He has done!

Thoughts of God

I have the breath of life, therefore I can overcome whatever comes my way.

You brought forth an army from all corners of the earth. They stood with me and we destroyed the enemy.

I have drawn back the veil and look at where I am now. I marvel at the beauty, promise and glory of the Lord. He gives me peace, security, sanctuary and love. Let me be joyful in the Lord.

I understand now that there are seasons to my journey, that experience and wisdom are life lessons. Greater things are coming; I can taste them in my mouth. All my disappointments have been for a reason and they can only strengthen me and press me even closer to the Lord. He who loves me knows the number of hairs on my head. He knew me before I was in my mother's womb and loved me first.

I have the breath of life; therefore I can overcome whatever comes my way.

Lord, look at the arsenal you have given me. Oh Lord, how you reach me. I have reading materials and music on my portable devices; so you can be with me wherever I go and share the gospel with others. These are some of the many great gifts available to me.

Lord, you have built a hedge around each of my children, husband and me. You always bring me peace and contentment to my life and guide me through all situations.

I Will Pray Tomorrow

I questioned you when my faith was weak,
For days sometimes, from week to week.
A failed prayer today, saying "Okay tomorrow,"
I am ashamed because my words were in vain.

As time went by still having not prayed,
My shame grew wildly, my heart sank in pain.
I could not look upon His heavenly face,
Lines of failure where etched in my thoughts.

Convincingly, I'd look up to the heavens,
Saying, "Lord I love you, I really do."
Please do not turn your precious face from mine,
My focus has slipped, seems like I've lost my grip,
Please don't allow me to fall into the bottomless pit."

Though my heart was willing, my spirit was lacking,
The devil knows when to come a-knocking.
Obstacles of delay the devil would place in my way,
Humourlessly causing my plans to derail.

But my 'Just-in-Time God', forever strong,
Plucked me up, placing me back where I belong.
Kneeling in humility, praying for his mercy,
Comforted by His Word, wrapped in His arms.

Sweet as the wind, my Lord Jesus reminds me,
"You have not failed, just taken your eyes off the ball."
He says "Switch off the television, switch off your phone,
Open your Bible and praise the Lord."

Warrior Power

Fighting through the battle that's designed to break me,
That cold guerrilla warfare,
The surge of fear that's fast approaching,
I brace my mind and stare.

Enemies' hooves speed towards me,
My heart increases its beat.
Tightening my grip I have to resist
The urge to turn on my heels.

Bombarded with fear, maddening my head
With the things that could happen to me.
Time to anchor my mind, draw on my faith,
Entrench my heart and be still.

I tune to that voice, so calm and clear,
That comforting frequency.
I bunker up, tune out the war
Refining my mind in Him.

From my tightened grip and my pounding heart,
Fear loses its hold on me.
I stand and stretch, my muscles flexed
Warrior power infills me.

No More

No more of the devil's food -
Pointless, twisted, bitter ghoul.
In Jesus, I have been well schooled,
Satan, I'm no longer your fool.

Thought you had me,
Probably stood a chance
The years you led me a merry dance,
Twirled me sweetly in your hands -
No more of your cunning plans.

Hear me now and hear me quick,
I'm no longer your next magic trick,
See my foot, I decide who to kick,
Now get out of my life and go live in the sticks.

My Purpose

The Insurgent is trying to derail me,
Constantly attacking my mind,
Looking to kill my purpose
And rob me of my birthright.

He mists me with fear and failure,
Uses people to come against me,
All because he sees my favour
That blossoms within me.

My purpose is not to make me wealthy,
It blesses those who can see
I have a gift, I share my life
To set the captives free.

I thank you all for cheering me on
And wanting the best for me.
I'll continue to strive
To keep us alive
With hope to fulfil our dreams.

Mind Trap

The Bishop preached a sermon
From a bible verse heard before -
Book of Luke 12 verse 22 -
Here's what he said and more:
"Therefore I tell you, do not worry about your life,
What you will eat; or about your body, what you will wear."
Jesus teaches this to us all
So we don't live in fear.

All of a sudden
I feel a mist of poison in the air -
The devil shows up and says, "Budge up,
Here's my version I'd like to share."
The next thing I know Satan tells me,
"Jesus didn't really mean for you not to worry -
We all have to plan, we all have to save,
So hold on to your money,
Don't give it away in a hurry."

Then the Bishop shouts,
"Luke 18, verses 18 to 22,"
"...Sell everything you have and give to the poor,

...Then come, follow me."

Half way through
Satan continues to meddle with my mind,
Interjecting, constantly pressing
Saying, "Let me clarify."
"Now Jesus didn't really mean
To sell everything you own,
Give some away, keep more for yourself
But please don't give it all -
You'll be worse off than before."

Satan's words of doubt and fear
We secretly hide sometimes -
Don't let him in, don't barter with him
Just pray for a renewal of mind.

All that Jesus was saying was,
Trust me now, come,
Lay it all on the line.
Do not worry, saints,
Don't be in a hurry:
I will always provide.

Night Time

Eyes wide
Doors shut
Night time's with me
Quietness comes.

Sleeping baby
Peaceful dreams
Heavenly blessings
Moonlight beams.

Think in private
Cry in sleep
Laughs remembered
Prayers for keeps.

Tomorrow planning
Thanking God
Smiling sweetly
Singing songs.

Breathing gently
Now at peace

Safely kept
While I sleep.

The Pain

Got a pain in my head
My eyes feel dead
A cold pole pierces my brain.
All from the blows to my head.

I thought I was healed
Alive, I felt free
My head was light
No more thuds in the day,
No more pounding at night -
Imagine my delight.

Out of the blue
In bursts Doom
Weighing on me
An anchor fixed and firm.

Clasping my eyes
I recoil to my room
There looms the doom
Into my cocoon -
Pain relief no time soon.

My energy sapped
The pain now gift-wrapped
This pain from the past
Came and hit me so fast.

Tablets can't control
Physicians don't know
All at a loss
Much to my cost.

My arms now give up,
Head hanging off my bed.
Jehovah Rapha, it's me again.
Please be quick,
Satan isn't missing a trick -
He's thumping me with his hellish fist.

My heart clutches for life,
My head settles for death -
If its left to me...
Well, you know the rest.
Only I can feel
What is happening to me,
I'm under attack
Too weak to fight back.

So I call on God
With a noose in my hand
About to abort
On my command.
But God draws his sword
Slashes my noose cord.
His shields are up
The heavens roar.

We call things that are not
As though they are,
We bind and remove them
In the name of God,
Then declare and decree
God's Word is law:
"Pain, be gone!
Go back where you belong."
Then God commands me
To get up and walk.

Strike Back

I'm in a season of my life
To take back all the things I lost,
The enemy will not win this toss,
My tactic's laid out,
The gloves are off.

Mission, enemy, troops, terrain,
All planned out in faith and prayers,
My Christian armour, perfect fit,
I'm ready and able to strike at will.

Visibility - check
Climate - check
The enemy won't even know what to expect.

What Was That?

Baby's nappy went splat
Then I heard "What was that?"
I leapt from my sofa to see.
Panic filled the air as I flew up the stairs -
Daddy and baby locked in a stare -
Who'd be the first to give in?

Daddy looked dazed,
Baby's bum wriggling in the air
Trying to get his little legs free,
But daddy hung on
To those little legs so strong,
Balancing baby, nappy and feet.

Seeing no disaster
I cried with laughter
As he begged me to take over from him.
"No way", I said cold. "You're on your own
And no mess on my bed please."

Aghast I saw him try to push past,
Holding only one of the baby's feet.

Wrestling broke out, but I won all the bouts
As he hurled ultimatums at me.
In laughter I managed to set myself free.

Out of breath and still laughing I averted disaster,
In defeat he saw to the baby.
To my delight everything was all right,
Our baby now lovely and clean.
See he did not really need me.
It's just a man-thing, if you know what I mean.

It's All About Me

Eyes wide shut
Soldiering on,
A woman's work is never done.
Hanging in there,
Could be complaining,
Still multi-tasking,
The family's asleep.

Pressing clothes
While planning tomorrow,
Time to sit down,
Hey, no chance of that.
Telephone rings
As I make school sandwiches,
Oh dear, I was planning a soak in the bath.

TV programmes missed
But I'm used to it,
Now my child has entered the room.
Mommy mode switched on:
"Tell me, child, what's wrong?

Ok, back to bed now,
Morning won't be long."

Texted good night to my husband -
His night shifts are long.
Collapsing in bed
Whilst conversing with God.
Drifting off silently,
Trying to stay awake in between,
Before a sleepy amen:
"God cover my family".

Flicking open my eyes
From my 10 second sleep,
How long was I out?
Did I really fall asleep?
Apologising to God -
So rude of me -
Pondering the day
That did this to me.

Again I thank God:
Children deep in their dreams,
Husband holy Ghost protected,
Eyes raised heavenward,
The house is quiet,
Central heating timed off,
Doors and windows are locked,

Blanket covers are up,
Whispering into the night,
"Goodnight, God."

Thank You

I thank God for my husband,
He is the love of my life.
He saved me from pain and death.
He revived my wounded life.
Though my heart was broken
He carried mine and his,
He brought new visions for us both:
Truth, love, hope and meaning.

He gave me things only hoped for
In far and distant dreams;
He lifted my battered head,
Encouraging me to believe.
He gave me the space I needed
To discard my pain, and me to him.
He waited ever so patiently
Until we both had healed.

He courted me like a gentleman,
Traditionally, as it should have been,
Asked for my hand in marriage -
Oh you should have seen him.

We planned the day of our wedding
With happiness, grace and speed.
God poured out tons of blessings
Beyond what our eyes could see.

Sunshine and rain, we married in May,
The rain on that day washed our past away,
The rainbow and sunshine shone upon our lives -
No more deceit to blind our eyes.

Our beautiful lives with beautiful boys,
Another addition, our bundle of joy.
We marvel at God and the blessings he's done,
He's kept his promise, our lives have begun.

Here's to our future, here's to the King;
Thank you, husband, for seeing me.
Our paths were meant to meet in this life
From ocean wide, from thousands of miles.

This time is ours to fulfil our dreams,
Explore, adventure, laughter to be.
No more heartache, only pleasure and faith,
Banded together, forever brave,
Victory is ours every step of the way.

Desert Storm

The journey you're on
Is a long hot trek:
For years you have carried
Some lifelong mess -
What's in your sack?
Does it give you relief?
Your hands are chafed,
Your eyes look weak.

Your words are bitter,
Your mouth charged with heat,
Your heart is hardened,
Your feet tough like flint.
Dispose of your junk,
You'll feel so relieved,
Your wagon trails littered
With things you thought you'd need.

Your eyes saw mirages,
The visions seemed real,
Heat became water,
Rocks grew truck wheels.
Come, take a look -

You've been carrying so much -
Start shedding the junk
Or just dump the lot.

Out from the desert
To fertile land,
Looking lean and agile,
Fit and strong.
Feeling much greater
Than when you first began,
Pressing expectantly
Towards the Promised Land.

All Is Well With My Soul

I can't help wondering why the devil's so boastful -
But all is well with my soul.

The eldest is crying and feels like dying -
But all is well with my soul.

There are sleepless nights and teen kids arguing -
But all is well with my soul.

Penny-pinching squeeze, knocking at my heels -
But all is well with my soul.

For I know my God is all providing,
He keeps my head up and my feet from falling.
Though the pace seems slow and never ending
Still, all is well with my soul.

Life is sometimes up and sometimes down,
There are valley times, then mountain tops,
Sometimes no, then yes yes yes -
But it's always well with my soul.

Super Natural

You're trying to entomb me 'cause you think you can?
I'm no detainee for you to tag.
I've been created from a Master plan,
To conquer whatever is in my hands.

I imagine you with your scheming heart,
Laughing and dancing, scoring points,
Plotting how you'll control my thoughts,
Auditioning my loved ones to take part.

But what you didn't realise -
Actually you were way off the mark -
My mind and soul are protected by God.
He built me up and mended my heart,
Planned my escape, gave me a fresh start.

Know that your arrows can't pierce my heart,
Destroy my soul or tear my life apart.
I'm alive and I'm free, anointed by God;
My power and authority stamp out your dark arts.

The New Has Come

"Hear, hear," the Writer cries, "I have a message for you:
"If anyone is in Christ, he is a new creation.
The old has passed away; behold, the new has come"[1]!

There may be "old" things in your life
You are trying to remove -
Maybe old habits or addictions,
Bad soul ties or your behaviour needs to improve.

A time of prosperity, new journeys and love,
A time for new friends, remove jealous old ones,
Make each day count, reject all loss,
Your faith and conviction are free from God.

Time to move forward, no looking back,
Spread your arms wide and joy shall come;
Let this year be your spiritual blessing,
Embracing all that God has promised.

Be encouraged today, no matter its state,

---

[1] 2 Corinthians 5:17 (ESV)

You have a chance for a new life;
Trust that He is leading you, all the way,
Keep His Word and embrace the blessings
That He has prepared for you!

Flourish like a Palm tree

Out with the old and in with the new;
Just like a palm tree, I know what to do.
Bent over in my storm, my life hit the ground,
As the violent wind stopped and I bounced right back.

What I discovered, while hunched in the storm:
He knew things would come against me to rob me of my joy.
He said, "You are a palm tree where storms of life blow,
But you're going to spring back up stronger than before."

You are wiser, more alive
And you are heading for victory.
Your brightest days are in front of you,
And nothing will hold you back
All you need to remember is that God is on your side,
So embrace your newness, smile,
And spread your arms out wide.

I Would Rather Be A Doorkeeper

As I journey towards your gate of praise
Love cascades from your dwelling place,
My soul yearns, my pace quickens,
For the courts of the Lord are near.

The closer I come to the open door
My flesh cries out, my heartbeat soars,
Inwardly smiling my heart delights,
My countenance changed from before.

For now I can kneel in the house of praise
Like Hannah and be free,
Consumed in love in this heavenly court
Anointed with oil that heals.

Just as the swallow has her nest
The altar is my home,
I would rather be a doorkeeper in my Father's house
Than dwell in tents outside His court.

Bless me, Lord as, I renew my strength,
My soul on its pilgrimage to you,

As I pass through the Valley of Baca
Behold, my tears make springs into pools.

Look upon me with favour, Lord,
Set my course, come see me through,
For you are my sun and shield, oh Lord.
I flow evermore to you.

Innocence of Youth

When did that happen?
My youth's innocence taken.
Sniper shots from behind my back,
This scary time came unexpectedly
And stole my baby's mind.

Children now having children,
Brothers still killing brothers,
Mothers stealing daughters' boyfriends,
Fathers absent through it all.
What hope for the youth then,
When Satan's roaming free,
Targeting innocent mothers,
Destroying whole families.

God says spare the rod and not the child,
Society confuses kids about their rights,
Some place in between a balance must be reached -
Who's gonna protect childhood innocence?
'Cause Satan won't give in:
His mission is to steal, destroy and kill.

All I can do is entrench my faith
And believe that God is coming.
In the meantime I keep my baby close
And tell him how God's wars are won.
My baby, I love him, my precious thing,
I've gotta hold him with all my might,
For my Saviour promised He is coming soon
To save us from Satan's plight.

What Would It Be like?

If ever I felt like running, the fields would never end,
the horizon lost in the grass so dense.

If ever I felt like dying, I could fall off a cliff and float to the
ground caressing the clouds or plummet like iron with a
crashing thud. Which one would give a resonating sound?

If ever I felt like crying, I could fill the ocean world over.
Do you think there would be no more drought?

If ever I felt like laughing, sound waves would echo without a
trace. If everyone did the same the earth could be filled
with joy again.

If ever I felt like sleeping, I might see gazelles leaping,
their backs arched high, slow motion in the sky, landing
lightly from their flight.

If ever I felt like praying, what would I be silently saying? my
secrets unveiled, inhale, exhale, heart beats at a gentle pace.

If ever I felt like fighting, would I lose my life for trying, or would I win with my victory flag flying?

If ever I felt like loving, would my heart be rejected or would it be tenderly kissed and be forever protected?

If ever I felt like dancing, my feet and my head connected, would be showing the best steps intended.

Good Day, Holy Spirit

Good day, Holy Spirit.
Thank you for waking me this morning
And for giving me the breath of life
You blessed me with a peaceful sleep,
Now I can start my day right.
I thank you for the strength given
To press on with this today
And in advance for tomorrow,
If I'm blessed in such a way.

I ask you for a renewal of mind
And to anoint me with fresh oil,
To remove yesterday's grime
And anything else untoward.
Dress me in my Christian armour
To protect me from head to toe,
For the devil's unknown wiles of the day
Remain yet to unfold.

Keep my vision focused, Lord,
Help me to walk in peace.
When I'm confronted by the ill-will of others

Let me bless them and forgive
For they know not what they do, oh Lord;
I pray they find relief
When things that are left to fester
Turn their hearts turn to steel.

I pray, Lord, for my family and people dear to me
I pray for those around the world
Who are worse off than me.
Thank you for sustenance and shelter
And garments you clothe me in,
This is the day you made for me -
I embrace the place I'm in.

Exceptional Favour

How could I have let my countenance slip?
How could I have let my faith deplete
Of all the glories and mercies you have covered me with?
My eyes could only be for you.

Just for a moment I did forget
That you can make bad turn to good.
Forgive me, I slipped, gave Satan a grip,
Flesh took me in its dark avenue.

When I came to my senses, Satan drew back,
He lost his grip on me,
My eyes came alive, my voice said aloud,
"In the name of Jesus, help me."

I fix my eyes on the hills
From there my faith comes.
In you, Abba, I cannot lose face,
In you Abba, I find peace, mercy and grace,
In you, Abba, darkness is erased,
You knew me first.

Blessed and Highly Favoured

This week has been exceptional, in that the Holy Spirit has been reminding me daily to follow through and press forward in the face of adversity. Though I may not understand what is going on and the way may be foggy, I've got to bunker down in the shelter of the Saviour and there I must be still and obedient.

He has commanded me to listen to Him and let Him teach me. He told me that my prosperity would flow like a river and never run dry. Which brought to my mind this scripture, "The Lord is my Shepherd I *shall not* want..." (Psalms 23:1 KJV)

In my season of charting unknown territory, I am confident that He will meet my daily needs, guide me and protect me from the wolves round about. They are at the gates, all because I am exceptional.

God reminds me not to be afraid, but to be wise and obedient enough to have Him lead me in the right places and right ways. He is my shepherd, remember. My proof is in the countless people He led in the Bible.

While I wait He restores finances and situations whilst dealing with other matters that want to envelop me. If the devil steals here, God restores there. That's how awesome He is. He is my multi-tasker. He bids me to take a seat as I am only able to do one thing at a time. He takes away my pressure while I wait and give me time for myself. He hasn't allowed me to get sucked in to matters He is dealing with. Nothing is too big for Him. I even have time to sing of His glory.

Today he asked me "What and who are you watching? Whatever it is, are you opening the door to the enemy? If so you'll become enslaved in the wrong thoughts. Keep my Word close to your heart, speak of me, talk to me."

All He keeps telling me is: "**Press on, exceptionally blessed,** keep the faith, and fix your eyes on me."

"Praise the Lord. Give thanks to the Lord, for he is good; his love endures forever." (Psalm 106:1 NIV)

On the Cusp of the Hill

How can you ask me to lead
When I want to follow?
How can I stand up
When I feel like sitting down?
Demands on me seem greater
Than the supply I can give,
Many people looking for answers,
Confusing my mind and pulling me down.

I'm on the verge of something
That's gonna be better than me:
A new awakening, new purpose,
A new season gift-wrapped for free.
I am matured by my experience,
I am validated with wisdom,
Into a place where I can be
Received like never before.

To accept my blessing
I have to be loose and free.
I curse the spirit of apathy,
Indifference and lack of expectancy.

Now I can understand
Why I was met by stormy seas,
The trauma, the tests, the wait
Where I stand on the cusp of the hill.

Is it why the enemy attacks me so
In this season of my life?
Can he see a value in me?
Can he see a blessing in my eyes?
Yes, he sees that spark that keeps me alive.

The reason why this test can't destroy me
Or the temptation can't take me out -
God left me here to seize the moment,
Behold, to finally grasp what's mine.

Am I afraid of what is before me?
Am I afraid of what I've left behind?
Am I afraid I won't be good enough?
I've got a whirlpool going on in my mind.

Then, I ask you Lord
If you're gonna give me something
Give me the shoes of peace,
Crown my head with understanding;
People will be pointing at me.
Assessing me like never before:
Have them take me seriously.

Now I'm striding towards my heights
And multi-dimensional dreams.

Lord, I ask you, give me wisdom:
What to do and when to do it
Who to trust and who not to trust
When to speak and when to hold my tongue.

In addition to the things I've asked above,
Advise me of the world's protocol
How to navigate the world interstate,
Where to stand and when to be still.

Don't let foolishness destroy my life
Before I get this new mind of mine:
Ignite my dreams, set my ambitions high,
Set my course and let this eagle fly.

Earthen Vessel

Lord how you used me,
Cleverly manoeuvred me,
To bring alive ears receptive to hear.

Holy waves rolled over me,
Words flowed from my mouth,
Eloquent and deep,
Who's this person within me?

Bursting forth this comforting gift,
My words resounding in their ears,
Helped someone's heart leap with cheer,
Holy Spirit, your work is here.

It's Already Done

Facing challenges and obstacles to overcome,
I'm keeping the right perspective; my battles are won.
On the right track and staying in faith,
Forward to victory with my flag raised.

Above all I know we serve an exceptional God!
Who pours out His grace, His wisdom lives on!
True to His promise and at the right time
He'll place you exactly where you belong.

This life we live sometimes leaves us discouraged,
But hold on to God, He'll keep you encouraged.
Your life is blessed, you're an extraordinary person -
In dark times He'll shine His marvellous light.

Keep standing in faith,
Keep declaring your victory,
Keep speaking His promises over your life.
Watch yourself go to new dimensions,
Watch darkness diminish before your eyes.

Tell the Devil

Though the storms keep on raging in my life
And sometimes it's hard to tell my days from nights,
There's a hope that lies within me,
That keeps me from the storms.
When the storms don't cease
And the wind keeps on blowing -
One thing I know, my soul is anchored.

You might see me bend,
You may see me cry,
You may see me stumble
But you will never see me quit.
I will fight the good fight of faith
Like you have never seen before -
My soul's been anchored!

Whatever life throws at me
I stand up to that thing,
Look it right in the face and say,
"I am not in this by myself -
God helps me, that's how I make it through
Come what may."

Absent Prayer

Absence from prayer
For how many days?
Caught up in time,
Chasing my baby blues away.
My time seems snatched -
I'll never get it back -
At times I feel we're both under attack.

I've lost my groove,
I've lost my song,
I need to get back to where I belong.
But how do I balance
Both bonds so strong
When my baby's sick and my power's gone?

I'll call on your name
And spout it all out:
Many times you've seen me cry and shout
Then you calm my mind
And rest my feet
You massage my brain with words so sweet.

Limitless

What a day, I am stressed,
I'm penned in, held under duress.
I really have to ask, is this a test,
As this saga continues its twirling mess?

Softly spoken words to highly strung ears
Have the ability to reduce me to tears.
Images of me in blustery emotion,
Unspoken words that should have been said.

I inwardly bubble from yesterday's blues,
Outwardly my countenance poised, calm and sane.
Thinking who can I blame for the way I feel?
Do they say sorry or should it be me?

There is no shame in asking for help
Why, their eyes are transfixed awaiting my fall.
I shall not crumble, nor show signs of defeat,
If I did, what would become of my family?

I need some rest, give me something for me,
Sacrifices I made for others to live.

How many desires did I forego?
How many dreams are yet to unfold?

Do I go unnoticed, unappreciated, or rejected?
Continuously I'm morphing to everyone's call
I'm not looking for glory, titles or fame,
Just a thank you, how are you, can I help you today?

Muddy Haze

How has my life come to this?
Resentment at the door,
Confusion at my heels.
Am I in my blessing?
Or someone else's curse?
Have I hit rock bottom,
As I swirl in a surge?

I have felt the worst -
Does the degree get deeper?
Here comes another surge,
Stronger than the first.
In my muddy haze
My heart screams aloud,
In my silent craze
I hold my head to the ground

Lord please forgive me
When wrong words fall from my mouth.
Do I fall to my knees?
Or place my hands on my hips?
I feel an upsurge of guilt

Which I carry around,
So I muster a prayer,
Whispers fall from my lips.

As I look up to heaven
Ready to let all rip out,
Can I come back from this?
Will He understand?
I'm in a quandary,
What does this all mean?
What of these things
That have beset me?

What did I do? How do I see?
Have I not heard
What you've been saying to me?
Speak to me, Lord,
Awaken my ears.
I'm all out of breath,
Do I care anymore?

Whose Race?

My bones ache from the toil they take -
I'm running but cannot win the race;
The tasks on me seem far too great -
They steal my time, mind, body and space.

Well intentioned people are all about,
Ready to advise and point out my wrongs,
Come, wear my shoes and see where I am,
My guess is, they would stand down.

If I'm wrong I'll say I'm wrong, I need not rationalize it,
Make excuses or stomp around.
Let me ask for forgiveness and trample this mound,
Get control of my life, turn this mess upside down.

My body and mind locked into a holy zone
Like a runner in their blocks ready to take off.
This race is mine, not for well intentioned folk -
Each step has purpose, my prize I behold.

Dry Bones & Her Staff

Whilst in my dry season
In the Valley of Weeping,
There came the Holy Spirit.

Parched and bleached from the beating sun,
Lifeless with hard pointed edges,
Protruding alone in the hot, glistening sand,
Sat the dry bones in a sun-kissed expanse.
An ornate still-life, my passing awaiting,
On my hands and knees through this empty space.

Thirsty, tearful, my face hit the sand,
Deep from within my last teardrop fell;
Then into the sand there sprung up a well,
Enough to quench the thirsty dry cells.
.
My droplets trickled upon the dry bones,
Absorbing my tears from anguish untold,
No longer looking brittle and old.
Up from the bones the Holy Spirit rose;
And gave life to those dry bones.

From my hands and knees my face arose,
To see these water-sodden bones.
My countenance changed, now humble and poised,
Exposed by my tears, look at those desert bones.

One bone I chose which became my staff,
Pressing me on across the desert expanse,
To palm trees colouring the clear blue skies,
To life, to purpose, reviving my life.

Not Today

He sees me here, he sees me there,
Seeking to confuse me everywhere.
Locked on his target, propellers turning
Desperate to snipe me if I stay there.

I'm on the move, continuous in prayer,
I cannot stop, my eyes a-glare.
A teardrop looming, awaiting my blink,
I feel the heavy weight of it.

But not today my hand awaits
To wipe that looming teardrop away.
My face transfixed, upwards in prayer
I call to God, Satan's target's failed -
Victory for me, in Christ I reign.

Us

You might think I'm strong,
But I need you.
You might think I'm dependable,
But you are my rock.
You might see me busy,
But stop me in my tracks
And hold me like when we first met.

You have my heart,
But I still love flowers.
You see me growing with you,
My heart is alive and vibrant.
I love you more each day,
My heart is with you always,
Forever true.

Noisy Place

The world is such a noisy place,
Hustling and bustling, no time for delay.
Whilst rushing, do we see the other face
Of the person passing from day to day?

Gadgets beeping, humans chatting,
Mechanical happenings in the background,
Screeching, screaming, ticking, clicking,
Items on standby, alarms ready to chime.

Amid these trundling, chaotic sounds
Can your body relax, can your brain slow down?
Most days I feel I'm under attack
From a tornado of noise to which I adapt.

We're designed to give one day back to God
For spiritual renewal and physical rest.
Exodus 20:8-11 explains this the best,
To restore and replenish, before your next quest.

Noise and fatigue sap your creative energy,
Distort your outlook, diminish your joy,

Erode your confidence and drain you spiritually,
No room for God, your body's shut down.

So how do you combat the noise we live in
That relentlessly wants to diminish your mind.?
Who woke you this morning and gave you life?
Give thanks to God, see your day run right.

Feel His presence engulf you as you pray
Your mind drifts off to His quiet place,
Declutter the noise that steals your praise.
Welcome to your secret and holy place
That balances your noisy world of today.

Confusion to Calm

That Chancer tried to stop me
From carrying out God's will.
I really had to laugh out loud
The way God swooped right in.
You really should have seen it -
It went from that to this,
Confusion to calm,
Defused alarms,
A peace felt from within.

Another day ahead of me
All in the name of Him.
Urgently pressing towards the mark
To victory across the hills.
As I journey I am humbled
How He always cares for me,
My steps do a dance
As He throws rose petals at my feet.

Stay Here

This lady here
Is drawing near
Feeling your arms around her,
Secured by your warmth
She melts in your arms
As your heavenly scent surrounds her.

Faint in your arms
She breathes so calm
Kept by your loving aroma,
Words so sweet
Sweep her off her feet -
You fill her world with blessings abundant.

Impasse

At the foot of the Cross
Deep in thought
I caught a breath of You;
No running back
To where I was last,
Still I feel I'm at an impasse.

Arriving here
I'm in gear,
But no way to be found.
I cry out, "Lord,
Where are you -
How come I'm here alone?"

Kneeling and waiting,
Rocking and praying,
That impasse and no direction made clear.
My poise grounded,
Desert all about me,
I wait for You to say, "Move."

Looking over those days
Seems so far away,
What you've done still gladdens my heart;
For You knew the purpose of my life
And point me to the Cross.

All For Me

Just when I thought
I had received it all
You pour out another blessing.
I'll never dry out
While you're around:
Your waterfall is omnipresent.

Seeds and planting,
Fertilizing, days passing:
As I'm nurtured and wait on You.
When the reaping is done,
The harvest comes,
Overflowing beyond my dreams.

Your ways surpass
What I understand
Only You, can do all things
As I fall to my knees
Help me conquer my fears
Make dreams appear crystal clear.
.

Slumped at the Cross
You knew the loss,
You paid the price for me.
You sacrificed all
So I could be healed
And have a new beginning.

Mr. Down Tools

I always tried,
You always gave up,
Quickly downing your tools,
Causing a ruckus.
The problem was yours,
But it became my fault,
I'd take the blame
Without a thought.

How you turned the tables -
That was so slick,
Bouncing over blame -
You never missed that trick.
Looking in your face
Made me feel so sick -
My day would come to see
You fall in your pit.

It was okay though -
I was used to your taunts.
I mastered it all -
Blame became my art.

I knew so well how to mirror you,
I secretly practiced in my room.

For all the years
I wasted on you,
All blame, shame and pain
You put me through,
I finally had enough of you:
You gave me reason to change the rules.

Oh how I've gone from strength to strength,
No longer cowed,
No longer bent,
My eyes never to be transfixed by you.
Forever I'll try -
What about you,
Mr. Down Tools?

My Plans in Disarray

Lord, I did not enter in your house today,
To sing, worship and pray.
My days and nights have been topsy-turvy,
My mind's been carried away.

Prepared and set plans to be in your house,
Saying nothing would stand in my way.
Those days have caught up so quickly, Lord,
My plans now in disarray.

My Sabbath is here,
Still I'm nowhere near
The gates to your fellowship place.
Domestic concerns, sleeplessness whirling,
Disappointment fills my face.
Annoyed I'm still in this place,
Repeating the same words again:
"There goes my Sabbath,
My fellowship praise delayed."

Saints of the house remind me, Lord,
Of an awesome service I missed.

That time has passed, nothing I can do
As I ponder and long for it.

So I sit here now, trying to clear my mind,
Hoping for a touch of your presence.
With prayers and praise in my heart,
I'm receptive to your Word.

Help me in this situation, Lord,
To make these crooked paths straight,
So it doesn't ruin this heavenly heart,
And steal me from your praise.

Awaiting your voice, that blessed timing,
Holy Spirit, come fill this place.
Absorbing holiness so awe inspiring,
I can feel your hands lift up my face.
From your feet where I kneel to pray
I whisper the word, "Amen."

Hate, Dissipate

The depths of hate our visions can dream,
Its hunger, its passion, seated so deep -
Into our belly it slithers, it creeps
Then out of our mouth in an instant it leaps.

In hindsight we cower, wondering
What was that all about,
As our voice bellows,
Heart choking our mouth.
Do we recall our feet leaving the ground,
As anger spews out with a deafening sound?

Lord have mercy, help us in our need,
For we know not how near to life's end we've been,
By a mind of the hate, embroiled so deep,
Hasten our escape from the murky deep.

We barely remember how it all came about,
In justice we tell of the suffering so long,
How we'll put an end to the hates so strong,
And put right how we feel we've been wronged.

That's why we must serve the Holy God
Who takes care of us when wrongs go on?
If we were to see all that the Lord knows
The enemy would be choked in their own sick joke.

We have a conscience, we have a purpose,
We can't be caught up in a mind so murderous.
God's promised us eternity
Not a life to be shortened by the enemy,
No longer entrapped in enemy hands.

Give your cards to God and not to man,
Play the enemy a heavenly hand
With God before and angels camped around,
You're undefeated, let your arms stretch out,
No hatred can pierce our heavenly hands.

Glory to Glory

To God be the glory great things he has done:
He is why I sing these new songs.
My mind is on a journey of where I have been,
When I opened my heart and invited Him in.

The times I've been tired, confused and sinking,
He rallied his Saints to keep me from sin.
They counselled and helped me, they never gave in,
My life was in darkness, no smiles from within.

While I was alone and my heartbeat was still,
I cursed, prayed and argued on who did this to me,
Upset from years that enslaved my mind.
His Words came as a healing, which now I live by.

Year after year the healing took hold,
Forgiveness and love, even patience would grow.
Forgiveness of people I'd dare not let near,
His saints, Word and glories enveloping me.

Then blessing and blessings outpoured from Him,
Too many to count but more kept pouring in.

Each month, year and moment were sculptured by Him,
He knew all the time where He wanted me to be.

I'm here looking over the countless blessings:
My home, my children, my vocation, my wedding,
My travels, my saints, my writings, my dreams,
All come from my Abba, His visions for me.

Today He has opened another blessing,
A step I have made to fulfil my next dream.
I feel all the victory of what will unfold,
My heartbeat increases as newness takes hold.

www.ingramcontent.com/pod-product-compliance
Lightning Source LLC
Chambersburg PA
CBHW031424290426
44110CB00011B/514